The World of Work

Choosing a Career in
Animal Care

Animal care careers include working to protect wild birds and animals.

The World of Work

Choosing a Career in Animal Care

Jane Hurwitz

THE ROSEN PUBLISHING GROUP, INC.
NEW YORK

Published in 1997 by The Rosen Publishing Group, Inc.
29 East 21st Street, New York, NY 10010

First Edition

Manufactured in the United States of America

Library of Congress Cataloging-in-Publication Data
Hurwitz, Jane.
   Choosing a career in animal care / Jane Hurwitz.—1st ed.
     p. cm.—(The world of work)
   Includes bibliographical references and index.
   Summary: Introduces careers as dog groomer, pet store clerk,
veterinarian, zoo keeper, and other animal-related careers.
   ISBN 0-8239-2268-5
   1. Animal Specialists—Vocational guidance—Juvenile literature.
2. Animal specialists—Biography—Juvenile literature. [1. Animal
specialists—Vocational guidance. 2. Vocational guidance.
3. Occupations.] I. Title. II. Series: World of work (New York, NY)
SF80.H87   1996
636.08'3'023—dc20   96-9453
                                           CIP
                                           AC

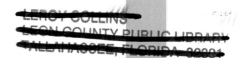

Contents

Introduction

Grace, Future Pet Photographer

I had all kinds of pets when I was young. I had snakes and birds. I even had a small bat once. But I think my most unusual pet was an African hedgehog. Animals have always been important to me.

I'm an animal lover. I consider pets as part of my family. I plan to use my love for animals to create a career in promoting animal care.

I work at a photography studio. I'm learning to become a photographer. After gaining some experience, I plan to specialize in taking family portraits of people with their pets.

There are many different careers within the world of animal care. The one thing they all have in common is that they focus on the care and protection of animals. These careers fall into two categories: working *directly* or *indirectly* with animals.

People who work directly with animals,

Most people in animal care careers have loved animals since they were kids.

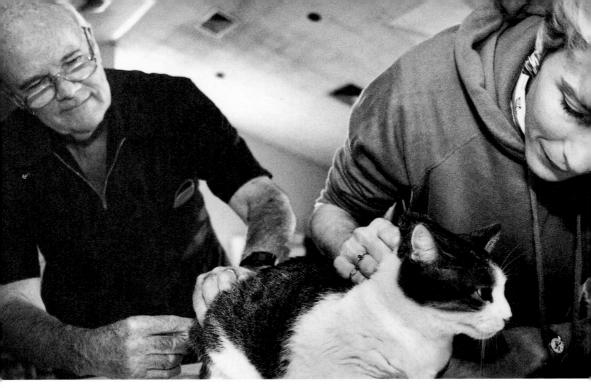
Veterinarians are doctors for animals.

caring for their health and well-being, include veterinarians, pet groomers, and zoo keepers. People who work indirectly with animals, protecting their rights and supplying pet-care products, include animal rights activists and those who work in pet stores.

People choose animal care careers for many reasons. Most people just love animals. Many of these people are happiest when they work directly with animals. Animal groomers, large animal veterinarian (those who work with farm and other large animals), and seeing-eye dog trainer are satisfying jobs for these people. Other people find personal satisfaction in

helping animals in distress. Animal shelter
workers, veterinarians, and animal rights
activists are ideal jobs for those people.

And then there are the pets. People who
live in the United States have more than 48
million dogs and 25 million cats as pets. They
own about 23 million birds, 12 million exotic
pets, and 340 million fish as pets. The pet-care
industry offers jobs for those who want to help
keep those pets happy and healthy.

If any of these areas sound interesting to
you, a career in animal care may be the right
choice for you!

Questions to Ask Yourself

There are many careers in which people can
work with animals. 1) Would you prefer to
work directly or indirectly with animals?
Why? 2) What sort of animals would you like
to work with?

The first requirement for entering a career in animal care is a love and respect for animals.

Career Possibilities in Animal Care

1

Certain attitudes, or personality traits, can help you decide whether a career in animal care is right for you.

Are You an Animal Lover?

Do you care about the fair treatment of animals? This is probably the most important personality trait among people who work with animals. It's also a good indication of an *animal lover*.

Besides loving animals, you must have a professional attitude that will allow you to function in difficult situations. Veterinary assistants often work with animals that have been abused. Animal shelter workers sometimes need to destroy, or kill, unwanted or unhealthy animals. This is called euthanasia. Animal care workers must accept these difficult aspects of caring for animals.

While many people are animal lovers, not all animal lovers will find animal care careers satisfying. Working with animals is rarely glamorous and often demanding. Cages need to be cleaned. Animals sometimes live in temperatures that are uncomfortable for humans. Taking care of animals' needs often requires long hours of hard work.

The majority of animal care workers earn modest incomes. Many careers in animal care require experience that is gained through low-paying entry-level jobs. Some careers even start out as volunteer work with no pay at all. Other careers require college courses or advanced college degrees. When considering an animal care career, you must decide what type of training you are willing to go through. You must also learn whether it is available and affordable.

Do You Have What It Takes?

There are so many jobs in the field of animal care that it may be hard to know where to start.

The first step is to think about your *skills* and *interests*. Think about what you like to do *and* what you don't like to do. Think about the type of environment you prefer to be in and whether you like to study. All of these things play a part in deciding what career path you may want to follow.

Answer the following questions on a separate sheet of paper. These answers can help you decide whether you should explore an animal care career.

- Do you like animals?
- Are you willing to be responsible for the health and well-being of animals?
- Have you ever done any volunteer work with animals?
- Do you prefer to be indoors or outdoors?
- Are you willing to get training or further education to work well with animals?
- Are you outgoing? Do you like to be around other people?
- Do you prefer to work alone?
- Do you plan ahead? Do you manage your time well?
- Do you have a good rapport with animals? Do you feel comfortable with all animals or with certain kinds?
- Are you looking to earn a large income?

Your answers can help you identify some of your qualities. Your qualities can help tell you whether you should work in the field of animal

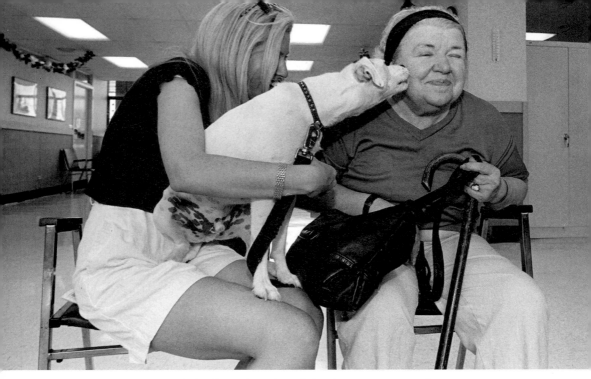

Animals such as dogs bring joy to many people.

care. They can also help you decide what kind of career within animal care may interest you. For instance, if you like to work outdoors, you may enjoy being a zoo keeper or a large animal veterinarian. If you like to work alone, you may not want to work in a pet supply store where you will have to deal with coworkers and the public. Keep your answers in mind as you read about the different careers available.

Johnson, Volunteer

Johnson volunteered with a group called Pets for Life. The group met once a month after school. Pets for Life took cats and dogs to visit elderly residents of nursing homes. Johnson enjoyed working with people and thought that was a good way to meet people. He also liked working with animals.

The nursing home residents really enjoyed the visits. The animals also served as therapy. They added excitement to the residents' day. Nursing home patients, who often feel lonely, cheered up at the first sight of a friendly dog or cuddly cat.

Johnson soon realized that his respect for animals had grown. He had always liked animals, but his visits with Pets for Life had shown him what an impact animals can have on humans. Johnson also became concerned about the impact that people have on animals.

Johnson knew that he wanted a career that involved being around animals as well as people. He thought about careers in animal care. He knew about veterinarians. He had taken his dog to the vet many times. He also knew that the animals at the zoo had caretakers. Volunteering gave Johnson new ideas about his future career path. How could he narrow down the choices to one career? What would satisfy his interest in helping both people and animals?

Johnson's next step was to evaluate his skills and interests. He identified his strengths and weaknesses. Then he decided that he wanted to own a pet store. He began by getting an after-school job at the local pet supply store.

Questions to Ask Yourself

There are certain attitudes or traits that a person must have to be successful and happy in a career in animal care. 1) Are you an animal lover? 2) Would you prefer to work directly or indirectly with animals?

Noncollege Careers in Animal Care

2

The best known medical career for animal lovers is that of *veterinarian*. But it is not the only choice. There are a variety of other medical careers from which to choose.

David, Veterinary Technician

I work as a veterinary technician at a horse hospital. I love it because I never have the same workday twice.

I start at 7:00 A.M. with rounds at the stables. I check on horses that are recuperating from illness or surgery. If an animal has problems, I make a note for the head veterinarian.

I also talk to the people who work in the barn. They clean the stalls and feed the horses. They also exercise horses that are able to leave their stalls. Since they spend most of their time around horses, they often know best how an animal is doing.

At 8:00 A.M. I review my duty list for the day. This list is prepared by the hospital office manager. Without a duty list, I couldn't coordinate my duties with the needs of the veterinarians. My list tells me what surgeries are scheduled and when. I also need to know the number of examinations scheduled.

By 8:30 A.M. I start to prepare for the day's surgeries. Most surgeries are scheduled during the morning. I make sure that the two operating rooms are stocked with all the necessary supplies. Then I prepare the horses for surgery. Sometimes this means taking blood samples or shaving the area to be operated on. After each surgery, I write up the surgery notes. I also file X rays and process laboratory samples.

After lunch, my work is mostly clerical. I order supplies and medicine. I take the temperature and vital signs of horses scheduled for appointments.

Every afternoon I organize and sterilize all the operating equipment. If there is an emergency, the veterinarians may need to operate immediately, even if it is the middle of the night.

At 3:00 P.M. I visit the barn again. I check on the animals that had surgery that morning. I look in on the other horses. If any of them need attention, I call the veterinarian scheduled for night duty.

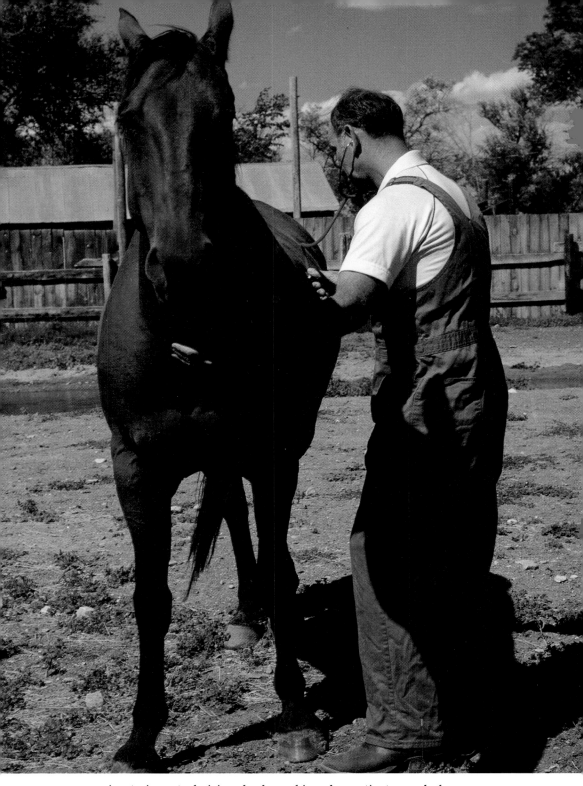

A veterinary technician checks on his or her patients regularly.

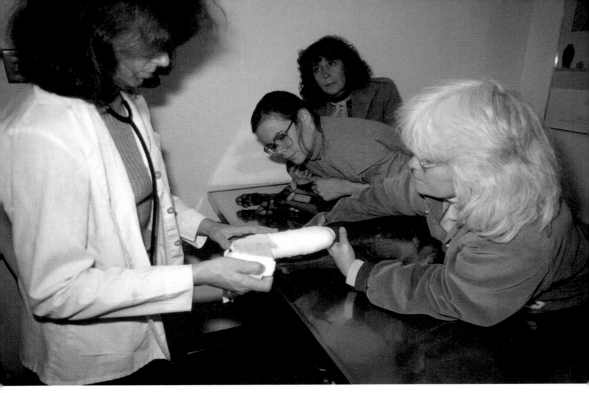

Veterinary technicians must be able to deal well with the sick or hurt animal and its owners.

I usually finish my barn visits by 4:00 P.M., when I sign out at the main building. I enjoy my job. Each day something happens to let me know that I made the right choice in becoming a veterinary technician.

Veterinary technicians do many things that veterinarians do. Their job duties include checking animals for disease, administering medicine, and taking X rays. Other duties include preparing animals for surgery and performing laboratory work. Technicians may also perform clerical work.

The training that veterinary technicians receive can be compared to the duties of a registered nurse. Like nurses, they are professionals. Also like nurses, there are some medical duties that they may not perform. They cannot make diagnoses, perform surgery, or write prescriptions. Each state has specific laws covering these restrictions.

Wages for beginning veterinary technicians range from $11,000 to $18,000 a year. Experience and education, geographic location, and size of establishment all affect their salaries. Technicians with greater experience and education often earn from $15,000 to $27,000 a year.

Other benefits available to veterinary technicians are health insurance and paid vacations. Retirement programs also may be available. The type of benefits for technicians varies with each job.

Technicians may be promoted to jobs with more responsibilities. Promotions depend on continued education through professional seminars, the technician's attitude, and on-the-job performance.

People who are interested in becoming veterinary technicians must enjoy working directly with animals. It also helps to be interested in science. Technicians must be able to work with other people as a team, since they may interact with other technicians. They are always under the supervision of a veterinarian, senior technician, or scientist.

To become a veterinary technician you must complete a two-year training program. To enter training, you need a high school diploma. Studying chemistry, algebra, and English in high school will be helpful.

Training programs are offered at *community colleges* and *technical schools*. Programs usually include working in an animal hospital or veterinary office.

After completing a training program, many states require veterinary technicians to be *registered*. Other states require *certification*. The American Veterinary Medical Association can provide information about these processes.

Part-time or *voluntary* work in an animal hospital or shelter can give you an idea whether you are suited to a veterinary technician career. Interviewing a variety of veterinary technicians also helps. Ask them where they trained. What experience did they have before training? Find out what their current duties include. Choose technicians who work in different settings. Consider those

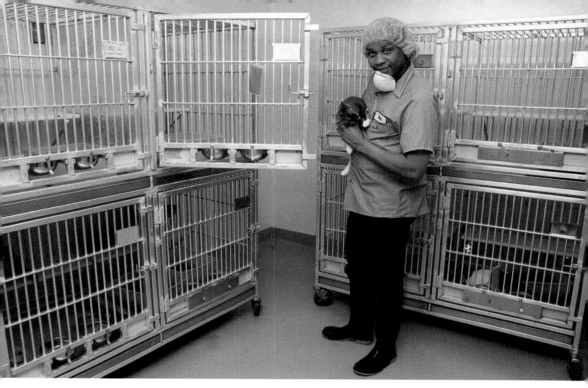

Animal care attendants keep animals clean, fed, and as comfortable as possible.

who work in animal hospitals, animal shelters, or zoos. Research universities, pharmaceutical companies, and breeding kennels also hire veterinary technicians.

There are many advantages to a career as a veterinary technician. Technicians have a wide choice of work places. The job often provides good wages and benefits. It is a professional career with opportunity for growth and advancement.

But the career also has disadvantages. It is a medical job that involves seeing animals suffer and sometimes die. If watching a surgical operation bothers you, then consider another animal care career.

A veterinary technician is just one of many animal care careers that involve medicine. Others include the following.

Animal Care Attendant

Animal care attendants perform basic care for animals. Their duties may include feeding animals, cleaning cages, and ordering supplies. Attendants work in animal hospitals, animal shelters, stables, and laboratories. Animal care attendants do not need a high level of training. Most receive *on-the-job* training. As a result, animal care attendants are not highly paid. But this job provides experience for a person considering a career as a veterinary technician.

Animal Production Technicians

Animal production technicians help breed, raise, and market farm animals. They work directly with animals on farms or ranches. Animal production technicians may sell or install livestock equipment. They also may work as meat processors and inspectors.

This career can be learned through on-the-job experience. Two-year training programs are also available. Starting salaries range from $11,000 to $16,500 per year, depending on education, specialization of skills, and geographic location.

Pet-Related Careers

Perhaps you are interested in working in a *pet-related* career. You could work with pets and their owners. Owning a pet shop is one example of a pet-related career.

There are many types of pet-related businesses. Some require you to work indoors and have regular hours. These include working as clerk, managing, or owning a pet store or kennel. Others, such as animal groomers and pet sitters have more flexible hours. Still others, such as pet-walkers and dog breeders require working outdoors.

Joy, Dog Groomer

I have been a dog groomer for five years, but this isn't my first job. I've always liked animals, but I didn't plan to work with them. My first job after high school was waitressing. But I couldn't earn enough money to get my own apartment.

A friend of my mother's owned a pet-grooming business. I worked for her on weekends to earn extra money. I learned about dog grooming and different dog breeds through experience. When I started, I didn't know a collie from a poodle!

After a few months, the grooming salon had an opening for a full-time dog groomer. Because of my part-time work, I got the job. My part-time exposure to the job made the decision easy. I knew it was the right career move for me.

I enjoy grooming dogs. I feel proud when a dog owner compliments my work. I was excited to start a career as a groomer. My dream is to open my own grooming business in the future.

Pet groomers usually work with dogs, a job requiring physical work. Combing, washing, and drying a fifty-pound dog requires a lot of muscle!

Most grooming shops are independent businesses. They are often called grooming salons. Most are open from 8:00 A.M. to 5:00 P.M., but sometimes the hours are even longer. Many people like to drop their pets off at the groomer's on their way to work and pick them up on the way home.

Pet grooming salons also sell supplies

including collars, pet food, flea products, and brushes.

Pet groomers also work at kennels and veterinary offices. Groomers at these businesses may earn more money if they train for other responsibilities. A pet groomer can also work as a kennel attendant or receptionist.

Pet groomers are paid on commission. Their income is based on the number of animals they groom. The average grooming takes an hour and a half. The charge to the pet owner is around $35.00. The groomer usually gets half of the charge, or around $17.00. To earn more, a groomer has to work for a busy salon or kennel.

Some parts of the United States are better than others for pet groomers. Pet groomers working in large cities, especially in California and New England, earn some of the highest incomes. Groomers working in rural areas earn much less.

Some groomers learn their job through experience. Others attend a grooming school. Most courses last three to six months. Some schools provide instruction in shop set-up and management in addition to basic grooming. For help in choosing a course of instruction, interview local groomers. Find out where they trained and what they found useful. Or write to a professional organization for pet groomers. Ask for their list of training courses.

You can also become a pet groomer by training with an experienced groomer. This is called an apprenticeship. During an apprenticeship, you may not earn much money. But you will learn every aspect of the grooming business. To find information about apprenticeships, ask local groomers.

A career in pet grooming has many advantages. It can be learned without formal training, it can have flexible hours, and it can provide great personal satisfaction. Groomers have a variety of choices about where they work. They can work in salons, kennels, or with veterinarians. Some groomers even work out of their homes.

There are basic requirements for pet groomers. If you cannot meet them, then pet grooming may not be for you. Pet groomers must work directly with animals. They must be able to control animals. Groomers cannot be allergic to animals or animal hair. They also should be able to work in a noisy environment. If one dog starts barking, other dogs will usually join in.

Pet grooming is considered a "pet-related" business. Other pet-related careers that require similar interests and skills include the following:

Kennel Worker

Kennels board and groom pets. Like pet groomers, *kennel workers* must know as much as possible about the different breeds of dogs and cats. They are responsible for the animals' total care while at the kennel. Starting salaries range from $12,000 to $17,000 a year.

Pet Therapist

This is a new field in animal care. *Pet therapists* work with pets to solve behavioral problems. Much of the early work in pet therapy has focused on helping cats. No standards or professional organizations have been established for pet therapists. The therapist should have a background in psychology and animal training and a strong concern for animals. This medically related animal career requires creativity and entrepreneurship to be successful.

Pet Sitter

This area of animal care is growing fast. *Pet sitters* care for animals while their owners are

Pet owners trust kennel workers to take good care of their pets.

away. The pet sitter usually visits the animal daily in the animal's home. Since they will be entering another person's home, pet sitters must be responsible and trustworthy. They must follow the owner's specific requests regarding the care of the pet. Salary varies widely here. Pet sitters are usually paid a certain amount for each day they watch a pet. Fees can range from $5 a day to $25 a day, depending on the sitter's experience, location, and type of pet being cared for.

Protection and Conservation

There are many careers that involve protecting animals and their habitats. Park rangers, fish biologists, and range managers are a few. Some zoos also work to protect animals by breeding rare species in captivity.

Elaine, Assistant Zoo Keeper

It isn't easy to get a job at a zoo. There aren't many zoos, so competition for jobs is tough. Many of the positions require advanced education. Other jobs are very specialized. I had to plan carefully to get my job.

My plan was to volunteer to work at the zoo, which I did during my senior year of high school. That gave me valuable experience. As a volunteer, I had an edge over other applicants, and I wanted to have the best chance possible of getting a full-time position.

My first duty as a volunteer was to clean the exhibits in the children's zoo. I also worked one shift a week in the zoo's nursery. I bottle-fed baby animals. I also learned how to mix foods for animals that were on special diets. I decided that a permanent job in the zoo's nursery would be perfect for me.

My volunteer work gave me great on-the-job experience. It also convinced me that a job working at a zoo would be a fulfilling career. I came to understand the zoo's concern about protecting exotic species of animals.

The zoo also works to educate the public. I saw that people learned from observing animals. More than ever, I wanted a job there. But there were no openings.

After high school I found a job at a veterinarian's office. My year of volunteer work at the zoo gave me the experience I needed to get the job. I fed and watered animals that were boarded at the veterinarian's. I also worked in the office answering the phones and greeting incoming patients and their owners.

Although I was working full–time, I continued to volunteer at the zoo. That didn't leave me much spare time. But I still hoped that a position at the zoo would open up. I wanted to be right there when one did.

Finally, at the end of my second year as a volunteer, the zoo had an opening. The large mammal exhibit needed an assistant zoo keeper. The keeper would be responsible for feeding, cleaning, and exercising the African elephants. Other work in the large mammal exhibit building would also be assigned.

Thanks to my volunteer experience, I was

Zoo keepers and their assistants take care of the animals' daily needs, such as keeping clean.

given an interview for the position. The supervisor knew I was a volunteer. My donated time showed her that I was committed to working for the zoo. And I got the job!

My work is hard. It involves a lot of physical labor. I haul hay and crates of vegetables for the elephants to eat. I also help bathe the elephants with a high-power hose and a giant brush. I often get wet or muddy and stay that way for most of the day. But working around animals as amazing as elephants makes this career worthwhile.

Most *zoo keepers* take care of the animals' daily needs. They clean the exhibits and feed the animals, many of whom require special diets. Zoo keepers also watch over the animals in their care. A change in animal behavior may mean that something is wrong. A zoo keeper must be a trained observer.

Salaries for zoo keepers depend on the size of the zoo and on the keeper's experience. The range for beginning salaries is from $16,000 to $23,000 a year. More experienced zoo keepers can earn $30,000 a year.

Zoo keepers must be able to shoulder a great deal of responsibility. They are directly responsible for the health and safety of animals in their care. Good communication skills with employees, with both colleagues and those under the keeper's direct authority, are also important.

The public sees the zoo keeper as an authority on animals. Keepers must be able to answer questions on animals' habits and diets. They must also explain the importance of maintaining animal species in the wild.

Zoo keepers are required to have a high school diploma. Some zoos also prefer them to have some college courses in biology or zoology. If you do not have formal education

Zoo keepers must watch the animals in their care for any changes in behavior.

in zoology or animal management, try
volunteering at a zoo. This could give you
experience that can lead to an entry-level
job as a zoo keeper.

The advantages of working in a zoo can
be enormous. There is a wide variety of
unusual animals with which to work, many
of which are of endangered species.
Helping maintain species that are threatened
with extinction in the wild can be highly
rewarding.

There are some disadvantages, however.
Much of a zoo keeper's work is strenuous
physical labor. Zoo animals also need care
every day of the year. This can lead to long

work hours, often on holidays or weekends. New workers often work long shifts for low wages.

There are many careers that work to protect animals and animal habitats. Other related careers include the following:

Wildlife Organizations

The World Wildlife Fund, the Nature Conservancy, and the Sierra Club Legal Defense Fund are just a few of the private-sector wildlife organizations. They are involved in *conservation* and *preservation* of animals and their habitats.

If you work for a *protective organization*, you will have little direct contact with animals. But your impact on these animals' lives can be great. The types of jobs available vary with each organization. Jobs include fundraising, public relations, marketing, and computer work. Working for a wildlife organization is ideal for animal lovers who are unable to perform the physical labor that animal care requires. Such work also has regular business hours.

If you are interested in working for a protective organization, contact them directly.

BALD EAGLE
WINTER SANCTUARY

CLOSED
TO THE PUBLIC

FROM DEC. 1ST TO APR. 1ST

DO NOT ENTER

THIS SANCTUARY HAS BEEN ESTABLISHED TO
ASSIST IN THE RESTORATION OF THE BALD EAGLE
TO THE HUDSON VALLEY.
IT IS CRITICAL TO THE WELFARE OF THESE
BIRDS THAT THEY ARE NOT DISTURBED.

YOU MAY VIEW THE BIRDS FROM A PARKING
AREA ON ROUTE 6 DIRECTLY ACROSS THE
RIVER.

thank you for your cooperation

A bird sanctuary is a safe place for birds to live. Someone who works for a wildlife organization may help raise money to help run things like bird sanctuaries.

Each organization has its own job requirements. As with zoo careers, volunteering is a
good way to gain experience that can lead to
full-time employment. Salaries range from
$12,000 to $35,000.

Animal Shelters

Animal shelter workers enforce local animal
control laws. They rescue animals and control
stray or unwanted animals. They investigate
complaints of animal abuse. Animal shelter
workers may be called to testify in court in
abuse cases.

Like zoo keepers, animal shelter workers
help animals directly. They are responsible for
animals' health. They also deal with hurt or
sick animals. Since the pet population is so
large, animal shelter workers see animals die
every day, which can be hard to take.

Animal shelter workers are required to
have a high school education. Additional
education increases the type of work available.
Salaries range from $12,000 to $22,000.

Questions to Ask Yourself

There are many ways to work with animals. 1) How
can you gain experience in working with animals?
2) Where can you find these opportunities?

Careers in Animal Care That Require a College Degree

3

A college education takes time, money, and a lot of hard work. The benefits of such investments include:

- Increased knowledge of animals and their habits
- Increased career opportunities
- Increased salary potential
- Increased prestige

Veterinary Medicine

There are many types of *veterinary medicine. Small animal vets* work with dogs, cats, rodents, birds, and reptiles. *Large animal vets* work with farm animals, race horses, and larger zoo animals.

Like medical doctors, veterinarians can also specialize in certain areas. Some vets study just a small aspect of animal health. Others specialize in just one animal. Veterinary medicine includes such specialists as the following:

It can be just as difficult to get into a school for veterinary medicine as it is to get into medical school.

- *Veterinary ophthalmologists*, who are animal eye specialists
- *Veterinary toxicologists,* who study animal disease in a laboratory setting
- *Equine veterinarians,* who work exclusively with race horses or on stud farms
- *Veterinary dermatologists,* who are animal skin specialists

Mark, Emergency Veterinarian

The veterinary hospital where I work employs small animal veterinarians. Veterinary specialists also work there. I trained as a small animal veterinarian, but I am also a specialist. My area of expertise is emergency medicine.

I began work at the animal hospital right after graduating from veterinary school. I worked regular hours during the week for two years. I also worked weekends when I needed extra money.

The only animals admitted on weekends are emergencies. Treating emergency cases was a challenge for me at first. Sometimes two hurt animals were brought in at the same time. Other times, an animal with confusing symptoms would be brought in.

During my third year, I was able to change my schedule. I worked twenty hours during the

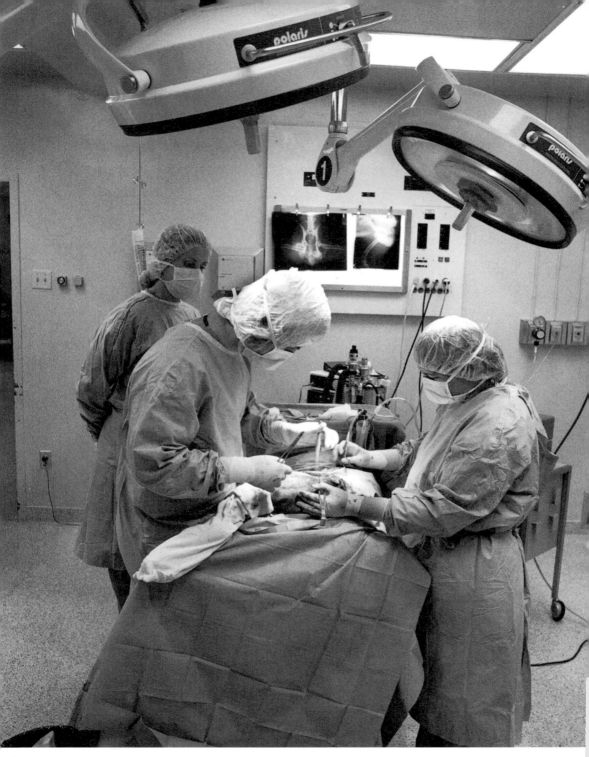

Veterinarians can specialize in different areas of veterinary medicine, such as surgery.

week. During this time, I saw regular cases, mostly cats and dogs. I also worked twenty hours on the weekend. That is when I trained to be a specialist—an emergency room veterinarian.

In the emergency room, I treat animals that have eaten poison or have been hit by cars. I also treat animals that are suffering from disease. Together with veterinary technicians I work to stabilize these sick or injured animals.

Ideally, an animal brought into the emergency hospital will be able to go home after the weekend. It is less expensive for the animal's owner to have the animal treated outside of the emergency hospital.

Veterinarians do a wide variety of jobs. They examine animals, treat emergencies, and perform operations. Some work in laboratories doing research rather than directly with animals. But they all work to improve the health of animals.

A veterinarian assumes a lot of responsibility, so the salary for this job can be quite high. Graduates start at about $15,000 to $25,000 per year. After gaining experience, a veterinarian's salary can reach $35,000 to $65,000 or more per year.

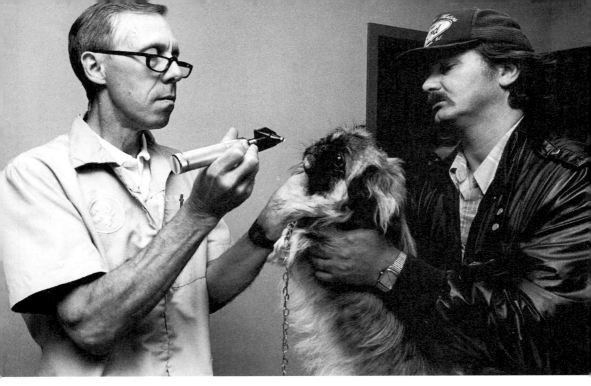
Veterinarians work to maintain the health of the animals they treat.

People who choose to become veterinarians must be able to work under stress. They often work long hours. Veterinarians also need curious minds. They must always increase their understanding of animal anatomy and disease. They need to keep up on new techniques and discoveries by reading veterinary periodicals and attending professional conferences.

Seventy percent of American veterinarians are in private practice. It is important for vets to be able to communicate well with their patients' owners. Pet owners expect a vet to explain their pet's problems clearly. To build a successful practice, vets also need to know how to run a business.

It takes a lot of dedication to become a veterinarian. First you must complete high school. Then you must earn two college degrees. The first degree is either a bachelor of arts or bachelor of science from a four-year college. The second degree is one of veterinary medicine. You can earn that degree only from a school of veterinary medicine. These are usually three-year programs. They are sometimes more difficult to get accepted into than medical school.

Planning for a career as a veterinarian can begin in high school. You can prepare for college by taking classes in biology, chemistry, and math. Four years of high school English will help with your communication skills. Business classes such as bookkeeping also are helpful should you decide to open your own practice.

It can be difficult to get into veterinary school. Once there, the hours are long and demanding. However, for those who are accepted and those who last through the training, a career as a veterinarian is satisfying and fulfilling. Veterinarians earn more money than animal care workers without college degrees. They also have more job options available.

Other Animal-Related Careers

There are other animal-related careers that require a college education. *Wildlife biologists* and *zoo curators*, those who oversee zoos, are two such careers. They both require at least an undergraduate college degree in an area such as zoology, ecology, or biology. While many animal-related professions require a graduate degree, there are satisfying careers in all aspects of animal care.

Questions to Ask Yourself

Animal care careers that require a college degree can be rewarding both emotionally and financially. 1) How important is earning a high salary to you? 2) Are you willing to devote the time necessary to earn a degree in an area of animal care?

Planning and Preparing for a Career in Animal Care

4

Planning is an important part of any career. Planning helps you focus on a career that best fits your interests and skills.

Preparation follows careful planning. Career preparation involves finding the right type of training or education and talking with people who work in the career you have chosen to explore.

Planning a Career

Planning and choosing a career is an important and often difficult process. You need to be honest with yourself about your skills and interests. When your job goals are clearly defined, you will be able to find a career that will be satisfying.

Now that you've narrowed your career choices down to a career in animal care, how do you choose which type of animal care? The questions in chapter 1 can help you narrow down the choices. Keep those answers in mind

You might try out a career in animal care by starting a dog-walking service.

while you read the following planning survey, which will help you pinpoint the best animal care career for you.

Planning Survey

Planning a career requires a close match between interests, skills, and available jobs. The following outline is a good first step in planning a career in animal care.

Careers working directly with animals and being responsible for their care:
 Veterinarian and veterinary assistant
 Animal groomer

Animal or kennel attendant
Animal trainer
Zoo exhibit curator (zoo keeper)
Pet sitter
Pet walker

Careers that require working outside:
Zoo keeper
Animal trainer
Pet walker

Careers that require working inside:
Animal groomer
Animal shelter worker
Veterinarian and veterinary assistant
Animal or kennel attendant
Pet sitter
Pet store clerk, manager, and owner

Careers that require the ability to work with other people:
Pet store clerk, manager, and owner
Veterinarian and veterinary assistant
Animal rights activist

Careers that may require less contact with people:
Animal or kennel attendant
Animal trainer
Animal groomer

Animal artist
Pet sitter
Pet walker

Careers that require further education:
Veterinarian
Conservationist
Zoo curator

Unusual Careers

Sometimes people with unusual skills or experiences create their own careers or businesses. These people are called *entrepreneurs*. There are many possibilities in animal care for entrepreneurs. A few examples are:

- Animal transportation or animal taxis
- Breeding endangered animals
- Pet photographer
- Pet therapist

Once you decide which areas interest you, follow up on your hard work and soul–searching by talking to people in those careers. They can tell you how they became interested in the career, what they like about it, what they don't like about it, and how to get more information about it.

Dog grooming might be a good career for someone who likes to work directly with animals.

Jack, Entrepreneur

During his senior year of high school, Jack began to worry. Most of his friends had career plans. They knew what they wanted to do after high school. But Jack had no idea what he wanted to do. How could he decide? He didn't have a plan.

Jack had never had a job or volunteered his time anywhere. He spent most of his free time working on his hobby. He was an amateur woodworker.

Most of Jack's projects had been gifts for friends or relatives. He had never considered using his skills as a career. But when he delivered a doghouse to his aunt, she gave him an idea.

"This doghouse is beautiful!" exclaimed Jack's aunt. "Are they hard to make? You could easily sell them."

Jack's aunt loved pets. She bought all kinds of things for her dogs. She knew what was available at pet stores. She had never seen anything quite like Jack's doghouse at any store.

Jack thought about the idea of using his woodworking skills for a career. Making specialty doghouses for pet lovers would be fun.

As a veterinarian, you may care for animals that have a large impact on peoples lives, such as this guide dog. A guide dog helps a blind person get safely from place to place.

Jack started to plan a business to manufacture doghouses. He made a list of his skills. He also listed skills needed to achieve his goal. Once his list was complete, Jack was excited.

Building up a new business would take time and patience. But with his plan, Jack felt confident. He finally knew where he was going!

Preparing for an Animal Care Career

Exposure to a specific job is a type of career preparation. Are you interested in working with abandoned animals? Then *volunteer* at a nearby animal shelter. You will get a sense of what the job is really like. Your volunteer experience may show you that working at an animal shelter is perfect for you. You can then plan how to become a full-time employee.

Working during a *summer break* or *vacation* is another way of exploring a career. Some animal care businesses hire temporary employees during busy seasons. Kennels often need help during summer vacations. You can tell pretty quickly if you are suited for a certain career.

Research is another form of career preparation. Public libraries have in-depth books on certain animal care careers. You can also write to professional organizations. See "For More Information" at the back of this book for some ideas. Professional organizations can provide information about education and training needed in certain careers. For example, if you are interested in becoming a pet groomer, write to International Professional Groomers. You can also check animal-related publications. Magazines such as *Cat Fancy* feature advertisements for training facilities. Ads often include schools for animal grooming and veterinary technicians.

All this work will be well worth the effort when it helps you begin a career that you love.

Questions to Ask Yourself

Choosing a particular career within animal care may be difficult. 1) Have you been honest with yourself about your skills, interests, likes, and dis-likes? 2) How can you find more information about the career you are interested in?

Getting Started in Animal Care

5

Now that you know which direction you want to take, you need to know how to reach your goal of getting a job in the field. One way is through volunteering, the way Elaine, the assistant zoo keeper did. Another is to apply for a job directly. You can find job listings in industry magazines, the classified section of local newspapers, and by inquiring at local vendors such as pet stores, veterinarian offices, groomers, and zoos. You might also try contacting the organizations listed at the back of this book for more tips on job-hunting in a particular field.

Once you've located a few job openings, you must apply for those jobs. To do this you must have the required education, some skills in the area, and a knockout *résumé*.

Your Résumé

A résumé, French for "summary," is a written summary of your education, work history, training, and skills. A résumé is usually requested when you apply for a job. It is your chance to make a good first impression.

Your résumé shows you have planned for a career. If you don't have work experience, highlight your volunteer experience. Any related hobby or school club can also be listed.

Review your résumé several times to make sure you have included the information you think is important and have recorded it accurately. The final version of your résumé should be typed neatly on good paper.

Once you've turned in your résumé and application, you may be called for an *interview*, the final step in getting a job. There are many books on proper interviewing techniques. You can study up on some of them by checking out those books at the library.

Getting a job is a lot of work. But when you consider that you spend one third of your life working, it's worth the effort it takes to find a career that you love.

Questions to Ask Yourself

There are several methods for finding a job. 1) Where can you find the classifieds in your local paper? 2) What sort of animal care facilities are in your community? 3) How can you contact them?

Glossary

animal rights activists   People who work to save animals who need protection.

apprenticeship   Training with someone experienced.

commission   Income earned based on the amount of work done or products sold.

conservation   Protection from the loss of something.

curator   Person in charge of a zoo.

emergency   Time of sudden need.

endangered species   Animal breeds that are being destroyed in the wild.

entrepreneurs   People who create their own careers or businesses.

euthanasia   Destroying or killing unwanted or dying animals.

grooming   Caring for the physical appearance of an animal.

preservation   Keeping safe from destruction.

rapport   Relationship; communication.

résumé   Summary of education, skills, and experience.

salary   Specified amount of money earned per year.

surgery   Treating diseases or medical problems by operations.

technician   Person who helps the professional in a given field.

veterinarian   Medical doctor for animals.

volunteer   To work for free to learn a job.

For More Information

The following organizations can provide information on particular careers:

Animal Conservation
Sierra Club Legal Defense Fund
2044 Fillmore Street
San Francisco, CA 94115

World Wildlife Fund & The Conservation
  Foundation, Inc.
1250 Twenty-fourth Street NW
Washington, DC 20037

The Nature Conservancy
1814 North Lynn Street
Arlington, VA 22209

Animal Protection & Animal Shelters
The Humane Society of the United States
2100 L Street NW
Washington, DC 20240

ASPCA Animal Rescue
2336 Linden Boulevard
Brooklyn, NY 11208

Pet Groomers
International Professional Groomers
79 Flint Locke Drive
Duxbury, MA 02332

National Dog Groomers Association of
 America
Box 101
Clark, PA 16113

Pet Sitters
National Association of Pet Sitters
1020 Brookstown Avenue, Suite 3
Winston-Salem, NC 27101

Veterinarian & Veterinary Assistant
American Veterinary Medical Association
930 North Meacham Road
Schaumburg, IL 60196

Association of American Veterinary Medical
 Colleges
1101 Vermont Avenue NW
Washington, DC 20005

Zoo Keepers
American Association of Zoo Keepers
635 Gage Boulevard
Topeka, KS 66606

For Further Reading

Brown, Fern G. *Behind the Scenes at the Horse Hospital.* Chicago: Albert Whitman & Company, 1981.

Lee, Mary Price, and Lee, Richard S. *Opportunities in Animal and Pet Care Careers.* Lincolnwood, IL: NTC Publishing Group, 1994.

Miller, Louise. *Animals.* Lincolnwood, IL: VGM Career Horizons, 1994.

——*Careers for Animal Lovers & Other Zoological Types.* Lincolnwood, IL: NTC Publishing Group, 1991.

Paige, David. *A Day in the Life of a Zoo Veterinarian.* Mahwah, NJ: Troll Associates, 1985.

Shorto, Russell. *Careers for Animal Lovers.* Brookfield, CT: Millbrook Press, 1992.

Smith, Roland. *Inside the Zoo Nursery.* New York: Cobblehill Books (Dutton), 1993.

Index

A
American Veterinary Medical
    Association, 22
animal abuse, 11, 38
animal care attendant, 24
animal production technician,
    24–25
animal rights activist, 8, 49
animal shelter worker, 9, 38, 54
animal taxis, 50
animal trainer, 49
animals, basic care of, 24, 34
animals, rare, 31
apprenticeship, 28

B
behavior, animal, 29, 34
biologist, 31, 46
breeder, dog, 25
business skills, 45, 54

C
career planning, 12–14, 47–55
community college, training avail-
    able at, 22
conservation, 31, 36
curator, zoo, 46

D
dermatologist, veterinary, 41
dog grooming, 25–29

E
emergency care, 41–43
endangered species, 35
entrepreneurs, 29, 50, 52–54
euthanasia, 11, 38

F
fundraising, 36

G
groomer, pet, 8, 25–29, 55

I
income, 12
indoors, careers working, 49
interests, 12–14
International Professional
    Groomers, 55

J
jobs, hunting, 56
job interview, 57

K
kennels, 25
kennel worker, 29, 54

L
laboratories, research, 43
laws, animal control, 38
livestock, 24, 39

About the Author
Jane Hurwitz earned an MA in Economics from the University of Kansas. She is the coauthor of *Sally Ride, Shooting for the Stars*, and *Staying Healthy*. Jane also is the author of *Coping in a Blended Family* and *High Performance Through Effective Budgeting*. She has always loved animals.

Photo Credits: Cover © Patti McConville/Image Bank; p. 2 © Evan Johnson/Impact Visuals; p. 7 © Jim West/Impact Visuals; p. 8 © Jack Kurtz/Impact Visuals; p. 19 © Kirk Condyles/Impact Visuals; p. 19 © Soble/Klonsky/Image Bank; p. 20 © Ken Levinson/International Stock; p. 23 © David Maung/Impact Visuals; p. 30 © Vince Dewitt/Impact Visuals; p. 33 © Jeffry Scott/Impact Visuals; pp. 35, 51 © F. M. Kearney/Impact Visuals; p. 37 © Michael Kaufman/Impact Visuals; pp. 40, 44, 53 © Martha Tabor/Impact Visuals; p. 42 Tom Benton/Impact Visuals; p. 48. Tom McKitterick/Impact Visuals.

Design: Erin McKenna